T0106219

# FROM the BOTTOM OF MY HEART

# FROM the BOTTOM OF MY HEART

## VOLUME 1

BY: SHARON HUGHLEY

iUniverse, Inc.
New York   Bloomington

*Copyright © 2009 by Sharon Hughley*

*All rights reserved. No part of this book may be used or reproduced by any means, graphic, electronic, or mechanical, including photocopying, recording, taping or by any information storage retrieval system without the written permission of the publisher except in the case of brief quotations embodied in critical articles and reviews.*

*iUniverse books may be ordered through booksellers or by contacting:*

*iUniverse*
*1663 Liberty Drive*
*Bloomington, IN 47403*
*www.iuniverse.com*
*1-800-Authors (1-800-288-4677)*

*Because of the dynamic nature of the Internet, any Web addresses or links contained in this book may have changed since publication and may no longer be valid. The views expressed in this work are solely those of the author and do not necessarily reflect the views of the publisher, and the publisher hereby disclaims any responsibility for them.*

*ISBN: 978-1-4401-6377-7 (sc)*
*ISBN: 978-1-4401-6376-0 (ebook)*

*Printed in the United States of America*

*iUniverse rev. date: 11/16/2009*

## Introductory

This book is to try to help women who get involved with the wrong type of relationship with men. This book offers a unique different approach of pouring your heart out and stating exactly how you feel at different times in your life and to recognize from whom your help comes from.

This book is heartfelt with the style of poetry; it states exactly what I was feeling and going through on a day to day basis. I am an authority on this subject because I have done a lot of research and I am also a victim of these circumstances of being involved in the wrong type of relationship with men.

Author of this delightful book is Sharon Hughley. This is her first book.

# TABLE OF CONTENTS

# DEDICATIONS/ ACKNOWLEDGEMENTS

GOD: To our GOD most high. Lord I magnify your name. With God and his everlasting grace and mercy has gotten me through some of the best and worst times in my life.

To my two daughters and grandchildren: For all the love and support.

To my parents: My mom for being my biggest supporter and friend and also for her eternal love. To my dad for telling me I am beautiful and can do anything I put my mind to.

My brothers and sisters: For all their encouragement and long talks about anything and everything I may have gone through throughout life.

To my grandparents: (Whom are deceased) Acknowledgement because while I was growing up they were supportive of my parents and supportive throughout my childhood. Just being the best grandparents they could be.

To my friends: For their everlasting words and encouragement. And also for listening to me every step of the way and being my critics.

To the Calvin's in my life: Had it not been for you and the life changes you put me through with all of your lies, betrayal, bad mouthing of me I probably would never had come to reaching one of the lowest points in my life to pour my heart out on paper. But God changed all of that and told me to draw nigh to him and he will draw nigh to me. God also promised me a future and a hope and all I had to do was reach out and grab it.

OH LORD WHERE WOULD I BE IF I DID NOT KNOW YOU

# ABOUT THE AUTHOR

My name is Sharon Hughley I was born and raised in Warren, Ohio. I was born October 7, 1964. I am one of seven siblings. I have two brothers and four sisters. Warren, Ohio is a small country community. Everyone knows everyone. My siblings and I spent a lot of time over my grandparents' house. Either in their gardens or helping my grandparents clean their home. I would not trade my childhood for the world. If we were not over my grandparents we were at home. My parents loved to have guest over and throw parties. We would either have winner roast, swimming in the pool, playing volley ball, or some activity. I was kind of shy around others but also very outspoken. I have always loved poetry-writing. My mom used to order Helen steiner Rice poetry books. I was so inspired by her books. So I started writing way back when I was just a child. At the age of 20 I mothered a daughter and then my second daughter came four years later. I relocated to Cleveland, Ohio in 1988 and have been here every since. I became inspired to write again when I came to reach one of the lowest times in my life.

# FROM THE BOTTOM OF MY HEART

Sometimes in life when we go through bad relationships we have nowhere else to turn. Well this was my story. I was in and out of bad relationships one after the other.

I thought to myself on several occasions! What did I do wrong? What could I have done better? Not realizing that between all of the bad relationships I had been through where did the problem actually lie.

I had to ask myself several questions. Was I the problem? Was I at fault? Could I be causing all these relationships to fail?

I thought to myself, "No I could not possibly be the problem it was the guys fault," but yet I was right there in the center of all of this.

So somewhere I had to take the blame on some kind of level but I had to figure out just how much was my fault and why.

Was it that I needed love so bad I was willing to just take whoever came along that showed me love that showed me attention?

Did I have low self esteem? What was the problem? They say that your childhood predicts how you will be as an adult. Was this true? Was my standard to high in the relationships? Or were they too low in the relationships?

I thought several times to myself if only I did this or if I did that perhaps things would have turned out differently. I thought to myself that maybe I had done something in my past life to cause all this hurt and pain on me.

I thought to myself maybe I just don't deserve a good man but deep down inside I knew I was a good person so again I thought what am I doing wrong?

Was I addicted to bad relationships? It always seemed on each and every relationship that something was missing but I could not quite figure it out.

Eventually I found myself unhappy in every relationship I choose. I found myself feeling depressed, stressed and unable to cope with work. Basically I did not have a clear head.

My thoughts were cloudy and unclear. Fortunately I did not turn to drugs or alcohol behind all the stress and pain of each bad, broken relationship.

I found myself physically and mentally abused through all the stress and drama of each failed relationship.

I don't know if I thought that if I ended the bad relationships I would not find anyone else or I just felt comfortable with knowing who I was dealing with instead of releasing myself from the pain, hurt, drama.

Was I afraid to be alone? That I would accept whatever some man dished out to me? Wasn't I worth more than that?

I had to ask myself these questions: Is all this stress, drama, pain worth me staying? Somehow I had to get to the root of the problem to figure this out. I knew I could not follow the same worn path that I had taken so many times.

Was I in such a high conflict in my relationships that I was willing to remain stuck? Was I afraid of change? Was I afraid to try again after failing in marriage? Was I a failure?

What could I do to learn to appreciate the person for who they were and not what I wanted them to be? Could I learn to prosper from each and every argument? From each and every disappointment?

For years I have remained clueless about what I needed or wanted in a life partner. I realized that once I got to know me and who I was as a person and why I made the same choice after choice of a bad relationship.

I needed not to just look at my life partners I needed to look at myself. Once I found out who I was, what I was missing and what I was in search of then I could find that perfect life partner for me.

I found that I needed someone on my level who wanted and shared the same common goals the same core values.

I had made a list of all the things that I wanted and needed in a life partner. And that list was to be my deciding factor of who I choose and why but I still needed and wanted this person to share the same common goals and the same core values that I wanted in life.

I knew I had to stop focusing on the guy and focus on myself and what I wanted and needed in a relationship or else I was going to keep attracting the same type of guy the same situation in my life over and over again no matter what the age is the guy could be as young as thirty or as old as fifty it does not mean they are ready for a committed relationship.

I decided I was just not going to accept any type of bad behavior from any man. You can't be someone's first till you start being first to yourself.

My main goals/core values was to have a man that shared the same religious beliefs as I do, this man had to be honest, be a communicator, respectful and wanted to be in a monogamous relationship with me, knew how to deal with money, be my best friend, be responsible, know how to handle and deal with important decisions and have the same beliefs I do about divorce.

Although I do not believe in divorce I know sometimes it is out of ones control if adultery takes place in ones marriage and the other partner can't handle it nor is willing to work on it.

I knew that if I had all this in a relationship that our similar beliefs and core values would be the key to hold our relationship together as a couple.

I knew in order for me to have a successful relationship with a partner that we both needed to be honest with one another. There is almost nothing worst than a lying partner.

Also affection is very important because is shows the opposite partner that you care, love and appreciate them and not to mention it feels good to be loved and touched by someone you genuinely care about.

Also being loyal to your partner and the trust you two would share means an awful lot.

I had made up in my mind that the type of mate I want and need in my life need to be able to build me up just honoring and preferring me just as I would do for him.

I knew that my next relationship would and could not be based on what he could do for me or what I could do for him.

I knew that we needed to sow good things towards each other. I knew that if ever I was to be married again I wanted my future husband to be willing to lay down his life for me just as Jesus laid down his life for the body of Christ.

I know that I would have to honor and respect my future husband, just as the body of Christ honors and respects Christ, as her Head.

I now know that me and my future husband must serve one another so there is no lack of love in our relationship.

I really and truly want to be the glory of my future husband. I want to reflect my husband's qualities. And I know that this will show if I am loved and cared for by my future husband.

When you lose trust things seem to go down heel from there. Also you should always make sure you spend quality time with your partner, learning and enjoying one another and getting to know each others likes and dislikes.

Last but not least I knew I needed a sort of unconditional love which I now know that unconditional love can only come from God but I do think that we as humans can certainly try to give it.

It is not always going to be perfect but we should try to love and accept one another for who they are. And agree to disagree and work through whatever problems or issues you two may be experiencing. Only if you are in a committed relationship though. Why waste time on a guy who won't commit to you?

One of the other things I had to learn is to stay away from negativity and negative people. I truly believe that what you speak about you bring about.

I started to understand that if I thought positive and believed what I wanted to attract in my life that it would come to me.

I believed I would not have to search that God would put that person in my path. I began to not think about being in a relationship and really and truly focus on myself and having myself become a better person in the Lord.

I knew that the kind of love which we all seek as humans is found in the Bible. Actually I believe in Corinthians 1 chapter 13:4-8. The Bible defines love as being "Patient and kind. Love is not jealous or boastful or proud or rude. Love does not demand its own way. Love keeps no record of when it has been wronged. Love never gives up, never loses faith, it is always hopeful and it endures through good and bad times.

I had to stay focused on myself, not give up and more than anything in the world I had to pray. I had to pray to God to release me from the hurt, the pain, the drama.

I had to ask God to teach me how to be a better person for him and for myself and for my new partner that I was going to attract.

I had to ask God to give me his wisdom, love, patience, understanding, hope, peace, joy, discernment.

I had to ask God to guide me and lead me down a straight and narrow path. I had to ask God to pray for all those who used me and abused me and to bless them and keep them always.

I had to ask God to show me what it is that he would have me to do?

Not once did I lose faith that God would not see me through each and every situation in my life. Not once did I lose faith that God would not see me through each and every bad relationship that I had chosen because he promised me a future and a hope.

God promised me that in my weakness he shall be my strength. God promised me that when I turn to the left or to the right that if I ask he will lead me down that straight and narrow path.

God told me that if he be for me who shall be against me. God promised me that he would be a friend to me at all times. God told me that if I have the faith the size of a mustard seed I could move a mountain from here to there.

I grew up in the church and had always had a strong faith in God but did I truly trust him?

I knew that once I had really and truly given myself, my life to God and not tried to handle things my way that God would put the right relationship that I had searched for my whole life

I knew I would have a healthy, loving relationship. I knew that all I had to do was trust God totally and completely.

God's blessings are bestowed on all who seek to be happy. Only true happiness is found in God which was another thing I had to learn.

By Gods grace and mercy we will receive his goodness. It is important that we seek God daily and ask of him what he will have us to do today?

Every good gift and every perfect gift is from God above. God is truly the source of all blessings.

Again I had to recognize and get to the bottom of who I am and why I made the choices I made.

I realized that after forty years of making the same mistake of choosing the wrong relationships that I was a rescuer, and also I suffered from co-addiction habits.

I also realized I could not blame anyone for the way I felt because my feelings are my feelings and only I control them.

My background as a child I was always looking for approval especially from my dad.

Even though I had a decent childhood something was lacking. Since I have figured out what my problem is I evaluate each and every knew relationship that I enter and if it does not look as if it is going to work out for me I end it quickly.

I don't regret or feel I have made any mistakes that are holding me back from having a good relationship with a man.

What I have started doing is gathering a sense of how compatible my potential partner and I are. And if we have the same common goal and core values.

I have prayed to God and released every area of my life to him. Each and every bad relationship that I could not fix, that I felt I had failed at completely and totally brought me to my knees and I knew I had to do something about it because yet as much as I wanted to blame each and every guy I had to take some part in this myself.

I completely focused my thoughts and efforts on God and getting myself in order to be the right type of person that God would have me to be.

Each and every day is a victory for me because I have truly had good days, heartfelt days, bad days and days where I just didn't know how I was going to make it through without the help of my Lord.

God is and always has come through for me in every way. He told me to take no thought for tomorrow and I totally believe him.

I know that God is a mover and a shaker. I today and every day give God all the glory and the praise.

# A Woman's Worth

Being single does not mean I am not a woman.
I don't need a relationship to validate who I am.
GOD told me that I am gifted and His grace and mercy
keeps me uplifted

I am thankful for GODS gratitude. I don't want do any
thing wrong nor keep a bad attitude. Being a woman
stands for so many things. We are worth more than
even the most valuable diamond ring.

Being a woman is so many stories that are untold. Again
we are worth more than silver or gold. A woman's worth
is more than any expensive item here on Earth. Being
in a relationship does not speak of a woman's worth.

A woman's worth is praying and taking care of her child. Her loving touch is so ever mild. A woman's worth is the support of her husband. With him she shall be his best friend. She will stick by his side till the very end.

A woman's worth treats everyone fair. She is someone you can count on and you know she cares. A woman's worth she is positive and to everyone her love she freely gives. A woman's worth she is content with her life. She is the kind of woman you would want to take As your wife.

A woman's worth does not like to fight. She would hold you and tell you that everything will be alright. A woman's worth would not use her sexuality. She would not give her love away to just anybody. A woman's worth forgives and loves unconditionally A woman's worth loves through all eternity.

A woman's worth is a virtuous woman she is worth more than the precious ruby and her attitude is wonderful and groovy. A woman's worth is loyal and will never cheat on you. She will love you till the end till she is actually through.

A woman's worth she will not hold back she will be straightforward with you and keep your butt on track. A woman's worth has no pressure. She is truly a gem and a treasure. A woman's worth is often sometimes independent. If a man is not acting right she will be the first to end it.

A woman's worth would not care about how much money you have she is the rarest of rare. She will love you and care for you and keep you in her prayers. A woman's worth in all reality she is the one with the loveliest personality.

A woman's worth you will know the one who is right for you regardless of her looks if she makes you happy and is down with you she will be there for you if you lost your foot.

A woman's worth is when you are feeling down in the slums she will try to help you work out all of your problems. A woman's worth is strong she will tell you when you are hurting someone and when you are wrong.

A woman's worth is often scarce. A woman's worth would not try to put you on the spot to embarrass.
A good woman would want to please God, and her family. A woman's worth is one who aims to please.

I could go on and on about a woman's worth but I don't think there is enough paper here on this earth.

# A day of life's journey

As I take a long walk down another one of life's journeys I consider myself lucky cause this time I did not have to involve my attorney

I know I have made some bad decisions I saw my life headed right for another collision. I seen how my life began to enhance as I made the right choices my life began to advance

With God beside me there are no more delays So I must give my prompt to God and to him much praise

# A Gift

A gift from God was meant for eternity He gave us the
choice to let our minds run wild and free

A gift from God who would have known that
you and I together is where we belong

A gift from God is such a treasure.
Getting to know you has been truly a pleasure No other
love will ever measure

A gift from God you were in my dreams
We didn't meet by chance so it seems

A gift from God from the most highest level
How could the love we have for each other come to
this to be so troubled

A gift from God could it be or did you just come to me
when I was feeling desperate and lonely?

# A good look at me

I wondered if I loved anyone dearer
As I looked at myself through the glass mirror

I wondered if anyone knew just how many
failed relationships I had been through

Then I dug deep down inside as I realized there is
nothing worse than having too much pride

So I went to seek a counselors advice
the counselor said your problem is you are way to nice

Then I thought maybe I just should not give a darn
but that would not be me that's not the person who
I am through GODS grace I have come way to far.

Even though I have been through these trials
GOD said he will show me my future and hope in just a
little while.

# A new kind of love

For us to meet was truly meant. Since I met you my life is really different. I want you to hear these words I want you to really listen. When I see you my heart smiles and my eyes shine with glisten.

I was going through a lot of changes and by my side you stayed. You held my hand and together we prayed.

At first I did not like you as much as you liked me but as I got to know you my eyes were open and now I see.

You were an man with different experiences. Now we have been together every since.

One day you smiled at me and that's when I knew. Actually that's when my attraction for you grew and my heart just knew.

As I got to know you and spend time with you everyday. You told me that you loved me and asked if I would be your wife some day.

Now I stand here before you citing our wedding vowels. I thank GOD for everything and if I kept my faith he would work everything out somehow.

# A Poem For You

From the beginning to the end I choose you
My only hope was that you had choosen me too
You were my love you were my man. If I had to do this
over again I would choose someone who would really
and truly be my friend

The love I feel for you was deep in my soul. There
was nothing I would not do for us to make us whole
The arguments, the fights lead to one thing or another
but all I wanted from you was for you to be my lover.

A true friend to the very end so I would not ever have
to feel loves hurts and pains again. I still love you deep
in my heart. I always have from the very start. And

this I pray you will always know even if I am dead and gone and ten feet below.

Too bad you were still looking at the closed doors. Now I am gone and we don't have a relationship anymore.

# A Scorned Woman

I'm still a queen and I wear my crown
A scorned woman in me is what you have found

I use to be nice and so attentive ntil you became so relentless. I know you weak men want to be the man that I am

And I don't care what I say anymore since you are not my man. I apologize if my words sound crushing. Seeing you cry really was touching

It's about time you got back what you put out. Now everyone will see the truth about you and what you really are about

# An old fool

Now I see what your character is all about. I can't believe the words that actually flow from your mouth

There's a saying there is no fool like an old fool. You running up behind folks who care nothing about you

Then when I ask you to do things for me I'm treated Like your worst enemy

Wanting people to like you for no reason at all. Does that make you feel like a man? Does that make you feel tall?

I can't believe on you I use to actually boast. Now your character is what troubles me the most

# Angry Poem

I really don't know what you are so angry for
You are the one who said if I continue to write
my book you were going to walk out the door.

You are not the object of my affection
If you really loved and cared for me you would have
Walked me to my car for my protection

Did I swell your head to make you think you were
All of that and more maybe at one time you were
the man that I truly adored

Because I loved you so much I would have gone
through the fire until I found out that you are really
a real big liar

You never gave our relationship the opportunity
to unfold lies on me is what you have told

I have forgiven you for what you have done
When you told me to walk away man
I really should have run

# Better Choices

It seems everything I touch turns into bad luck. I have to make some decisions so I won't remain stuck

I have so many choices to make so I don't continue to make the same mistake

I don't know why I am going through things but I must trust my Savior. I am the one who made the bad choices because of my bad behavior

I asked God to turn this bad luck into something positive because I have nothing left to offer I have
Before I have nothing left to give

Lord I need to hear from you. Lord I need to hear your voice. Lord please continue to guide me so I will make the right choice

# Big Ball Of Confusion

There is really no illusion. You are a real big ball
Of confusion. Always talking about what your
gonna do. Man I can't believe I had the nerve to fall in
love with you

I tried to lift your spirits on most high. Now I wonder
why I even tried. You are one of the weakest men I have
ever known. Sitting around listening to those silly
love songs

Its over, Its over, Open your eyes and see. Even me
who once loved you is asking GOD to set me free

# Change

Some people don't change you give them chance after chance and things remain the same.

They say Leopards don't change their spots they just change their colors. Nowadays people don't respect one another

People playing games and trying to use you for what they can not even caring if they take your woman or your man

I wish A change would come and all these killings would stop. I wish the world was not corrupt with all these crooked cops

A change is coming and it's coming today
I hope the change is here to stay

# Change My Life

God told me he was going to change my life for the
good. My first thought was "Thank you God"
I really wish you would

God told me he would never leave my side. He said
"My child its your choice, now you must decide"

I looked back at my life over the years and my eyes
began to swell up so full of tears

I said "Thank you Lord I am glad you have come"
"You washed away all my sins and now my new life
has begun"

# Closer Walk With Thee

Just a closer walk with thee. I am constantly under the attack of the enemy

You said my child come and take my hand. And trust in me till you completely understand

You must walk by faith and not by sight. Believe in that and everything will turn out all right

There is no need to rush and there is no need to every hurry continue to trust in me and you won't have to ever worry

I am the light in front of you shining so ever bright remember when you thought you could not make it through another single night

I told you my child I would be by your side. I have been there every step of the way being your guide

# Did You Know

Did you know that you could talk things into existence
If you believe in God and be Persistent

Did you know that God gives you your hearts desires
I learned this all as the bishop spoke and his sermon was on fire.

Did you know that God is the potter and the Clay
God can change your heart to be like him someday

Did you know that God is in complete control
All we have to do is continue to be faithful

# Do you

Do you ever feel like you are living in constant misery
or do you just feel desparate and lonely

Do you ever wonder why you break down and cry or
do you want a second chance to give things another try

Do you ever wish that someone would love you
unconditionally. Do you ever wonder why do things
always happen to me

Do you care if a change comes your way. Do you ever
take time to sit down and pray. Do you ever let people
lower your self esteem. Do you live life to its fullest
Do you live out your dreams

Do you ever wish our relationship we could mend
Or would you rather just let it come to an end?

# Don't Keep Saying

Don't keep saying you are going to call me
as old as you are you sound very silly

We are not children growing up in high school
so why are you making all these silly rules

Don't keep saying you love me so much but you
don't spend time with me you don't even keep in
touch

Don't keep saying that I am the woman that you
want. Your words mean nothing all they do is
disappoint

Don't keep saying that your mind is in a disarray
Don't keep thinking that everything between us
is going to be ok

# Eastside Church of God in Christ

Eastside Church of God in Christ is the church I grew up in. My grandfather led us to church and that's when it all began

Eastside Church of God in Christ is where I was baptized and gave my life to Christ before I even realized

My grandfather made sure we made it to church every Sunday then off to school on early morning Monday

Even though I live elsewhere I pray that members of Eastside Church of God in Christ continues to keep me in their prayers

God Bless all of you
Take care

# End of the road

Don't call me now and want to spend time with me because you are drunk. The way I let you mistreat me in our relationship just purely stunk

I thought you loved me but my heart only seen blindness all my mind seen was your financial kindness

For two years I patiented waited and just being with you I felt elated I seen it wasn't going anywhere as we continued to date

What was I possibly thinking you were already someone else's mate. I made a mistake and got my love all twisted. When you didn't need me anymore you just kept Right on and dismissed me

But that's ok I will fight evil for good not because I want to but because I should. This time really is the end of the road. This is the true story everyone first time untold.

# Enough

I have finally come to the point where I have had
enough. I guess I didn't realize being with you
would be so tough

Enough is enough and I can't say it No more
All I want to do now is walk out that door

Enough is enough I have had all I can take
I don't even like being around you because your
emotions are fake

Enough is enough you are always putting me down
Instead of lifting me up but I don't have to stay with
you I don't have to stay stuck

Enough is enough now go on ok. Don't bring your butt
back around this way

# Fallen Nature

Our fallen nature the ways of the world things were much easier when I was just a little girl

I remember so many deaths. Our fallen nature is what my memory collects

Our fallen nature is not a revelation. People are being locked up and so many people put on probation

I remember when there were family reunions. The world is falling apart is my conclusion

Our fallen nature must definitely improve. This is the only way to have a march of a freedom move

Soldiers dying everyday is there not a better way

# Go Away

Go away I don't want to hurt you anymore. I don't know what the future hold for you and me . I don't know what's in store

Go away I am all confused. You are one I really don't want to loose please don't make me have to choose

Go away I just want to be left alone I need sometime to clear my head and figure out where I went wrong

Go away I am so depressed. I laugh on the outside but my mind and my heart is such a mess. I am so afraid I am going to die from all the stress

Go away I just need some time to think I need some time to work through all of the kinks

How do I choose between twenty five years or someone that truly loves me so very dear. Lord I'm so afraid and filled with an awful lot of fear.

Lord help me and tell me which way to go my heart is very sad and I feel so very low Lord help me I'm praying my heart out to You. Lord please please tell me what I should do

# Goals in Life

Without a goal you have nothing to look forward to
I am here to say keep reaching till you make it through

Things are never quite as hard as it seems that's why
you have to believe in your dreams

And if you hold tight to what you believe in
Don't let no one stop you finish till the end

That's when your dreams will all come true
And you will have no one to thank but
God and you

# GOD give me strength

GOD give me strength in my time of need at one time
I was hurting so bad so I got down on my knees and
begged and plead

GOD give me strength to go another mile
If you do this for me I will be a better person this
I vowel

GOD said please don't make promises you know
You are not going to keep. You are the one who
Made the choices now your in knee deep

I will give you strength if you ask and seek
I know right now you are timid and weak

But I will carry you through snow, heavy wind
Or rain have faith in me and strength you shall
Regain

I waited for you for such a long time to come
Back home. I let you make your own choice and
You knew what you were doing was wrong

For I will give you Strengthen for your faith
Has made you whole even though it took you
Sometime to realize I am GOD I am the one in
Control

# God Grant Me

God grant me the serenity there's so many people
that envy. God grant me the patience isn't that written
in the Book of Revelations

God grant me the strength help me act like I have
some sense. God grant me the knowledge so I can help
get my children graduate and get through college

God grant me the grace so on this earth I will
know my place. God grant me the power so I won't act
like I am a coward

God grant me your grace till you come. God grant me
the grace to know where my help comes from

# God Is

God is a mover and a shaker
God is a giver and not a taker
God is the real definition of love
God sends down his gifts from above
God knows how to work things out for our good
God knows when we cant and when we should
God sends us his ever so loving grace
God knows every frown and wrinkle on our face
God will be there when no one else will
I hear a soft whisper saying "Peace be still"
Then I realize this is the path God wants me to take
And this is something I can not forsake.
Then I reach out and ask God for more grace
And his answer is "yes child for as long as it takes."

# God Told Me

God told me that quietness and confidence shall be my strength. This is something I can not go against

God told me that he that shall come will come and will not tarry. I know in my heart this will be the man that I marry

God told me he was offering me a future and a hope
He said if I get tired and at the end of my rope
Tie a knot and keep pushing up that slope

God told me that he was setting me free. In the Bible it means God is giving me liberty. God shows me so many Revelations. In God I trust he is my consolation

I feel the Lords everlasting power. I know God is with me every minute upon each hour.

# Gods Direction
# And Protection

At times it seemed like my world was coming to a holt even when I clearly knew situations were not my fault.

God was moving people and things out of my life for my protection as I made a lot of bad decisions and a life full of corrections.

God said if you follow me and do my commands you won't end up with me having to reprimand.

God said I will give you light and direction and you shall reign forever and ever. My child have you not figured out that I will leave you never. I am doing this all for the betterment. And to you my son I sent.

God said seal not the sayings of the prophecy of the book of the bible for the time is at hand. All you have to do is be obedient and just stand.

God said child my grace is sufficient enough for thee.
Follow my commands and I shall surely set you free.

As you obey me I will open doors
that you will not have room enough to receive.
And I told you child even when you have little faith I
will not leave.

And if you keep the word of my patience
I will also keep you from the hour of your temptations.
Because I love you child you are my creation.

# Gods promise

God told me my new man was coming
so I ran to the mirror to make sure I looked stunning

I waited by the window with such a glow hoping and
praying It might be Somebody I already know

As hours past and he never came
flat my hair was and I felt very shame

So tomorrow I will sit by the window and act as if I
don't care where the oldest clothes I have and this time
not stare

I see a tall, handsome man walking Right up to my
front door. He had on a suit what would he ever want
me for

The moral of the story is to always do and look your
best. You never know when God Is going to putting
you through a test

# Gods Wisdom

I asked God for Wisdom he gave me that and more
He gave me grace, mercy, patience and hope more
than I had before

I asked God to show me his Kingdom instead he gave
me more Wisdom. He said "Wisdom is what you need
first then I shall show you my Kingdom"

I asked God what does his Wisdom mean. He said "My
child Wisdom is greater than anything you have ever
seen. Follow me and you shall know my Wisdom and
surely you will reign as Queen"

I asked God to teach me his Wisdom and show me his
ways. God said "my Wisdom is more than you can
imagine and I will show you her beauty someday"

# Grow up my three girls

Grow up girls and get your lives situated. What are you gonna do when mommys dead, gone and belated?

I'm gonna tell you the reasons why because someday mommy is going to die

So I want all three of you to keep your heads up high And don't be mistreated ever by any guy

One day you all will really understand what I mean Make sure you are with a man who is really on your team

Make sure you always keep some available cash on hand. That way you don't have to depend on any man

Listen to me girls and heed my advice. Keep your faith in God and that should be suffice

# Have You

Have you ever felt like you did not want to go to your own home because you were in a strained relationship and your love was all gone

Have you ever felt that deep connection. And then one day you no longer have these same feelings of affection

Have you ever loved someone deep in your soul and you thought you and that person would stay together and grow old

Have you ever had someone you truly adored
Have you ever felt in a relationship so secure

Have you ever had a love like mine. I think not because I am one of a kind

# From the Bottom of My Heart

Women we all have internal warning signs which warns us that we can't and should not put up with a man who does not treat us right nor respect us. These signs are called gut feelings, women's intuition, or some may call them red flags.

Women if you find yourself with this type of man that is so self centered, controlling, unreliable- never does what he says and never shows up on time, if he is childish, plays mind games, emotionally draining, confused as to what he wants in life, or if he threatens your life in any type of way. By all means if you are with this type of man run for your life.

This man will damage your self esteem, have you confused and play with your emotions. If you have a gut feeling or any type of inclination that this guy is not right for you please stop dating him while you are ahead and move on to a man that will bring you joy and not pain, happiness and not frustration, peace and not confusion to your life. Find a man that will compliment you and your needs and wants.

We women need to stop excusing inexcusable behavior. For Example: I once went out with this guy it was our very first date and our first date was at a night club. We were to listen to the jazz band that played that evening. Well when I arrived my date was sitting at the bar. I walked over to him and gave him a hug.

I noticed several young ladies sitting at the bar directly across from us. I noticed that one of the young ladies kept staring at my date and I noticed that he would from time to time stare back at her even though I was sitting right there. I figured I would go to the ladies room to freshen up.

When I came out of the ladies room my date was standing at the other side of the bar talking to the young lady.

He came back explaining that she was a friend of a friend. At that point I did not know him nor did I know if he was telling the truth.

But from the time I got there I had a funny feeling already about this whole situation anyways. Well I had my back turned towards my date so that I could watch the jazz band playing but at the same time I could see my date from the corner of my eye.

I noticed that the young lady was about to leave. I looked at my date from the corner of my eye to see him with his hand to his ear saying that he was going to call her.

I was livid because I felt like I was being played. He was on a date with me but interested in another woman. What the heck??????

I immediately got angry. At that point I should have walked away but I cussed him out instead and do you know what I did next. Like an idiot I went out with him again and again. To just find myself hurt one by one with different things he did and said during our dating.

I had to break free from this so I went into deep prayer and asked God to remove this man from me. God answered my prayer. I should have never allowed this type of behavior.

By going out with him again I was telling him it was ok for him to disrespect me. I should have walked away from the very beginning to never give this man another chance to be in my presence.

He was not deserving to be in my gracious company. This man did not respect me from the start. That is the bottom line!!! And this is just one example of inexcusable behavior.

I had to look at the situation after I pulled myself together and realize was I willing to settle for what he was giving me. My answer to this situation from that point on is "NO"

Example number two: I once dated and had the nerve to marry a guy that was a mama's boy. I seen all the signs. He told his mom everything.

His mom did not like me from the start. She and her sisters and her mother would from the beginning call me his ex-wife's name.

I always felt like they were doing it on purpose, however, it could have been my imagination. Also his mother was always calling the house all day long and giving her unwanted advice in our affairs. This is only because he got his mother involved in everything that we did.

Actually his mother would not even come to our wedding because she felt he was making a mistake. Little did she know I was the one making the mistake. Women we are at a no win situation with this type of bond between mother and son. I was always second best to his mother.

Don't get me wrong there is nothing wrong with a man that adores and loves his mother. I felt like his mother was trying to control our life and our marriage. I remember one year for my birthday his mother bought me two tickets to a gospel concert. His mother told me that I could take whoever I wanted to the concert and of course if she bought the tickets for me for my birthday then that was my gift and I would be free to take whom I choose.

Of course I had planned to take my husband but he and I had gotten mad at each other and I told him I was not going to take him and guess what he did next? He called his mama.

So in return I got a call from her saying I did not buy you those tickets for your birthday so that you can take someone else. I bought them so you could take your husband. I was livid and felt betrayed.

I told her well you know what I will just pay for the one ticket and give you back the other ticket and if you want to give it to your son then you give it to him but I refuse to take your tickets as a birthday present if you are going to dictate who I can take to the concert.

That was just one example of all of the stress and agony I went through during this marriage. Fortunately for me he was a cheater to so when he said he did not want to be married anymore it did not make it any easier or ease the pain I felt but it was a no brainard when it came time to file for the divorce.

I thought about all the things he had done to me in the course of our marriage and was more than glad to be freed from the hurt and pain I felt during our time together.

I was more than happy to ship this guy back to his mama where he belonged. Since she played a part in all of his decisions. Also since he never ever defended me to her I figured he couldn't live without her and I was better off without him in my life.

Example Three: I dated a guy for almost three years. He was totally confused. His confusion came along with depression, narcissist attitude and he did nothing but disrespect me and talk about me behind my back.

Which I found out towards the end of our relationship. And he lied on me to everyone to make himself appear to be something that he was not.

During this relationship I was also confused, stressed, depressed, lonely, and quite often sad. I had truly loved this man from the bottom of my heart. And at this point because of some crazy, unknown reason could not break free from the pain and drama I felt during this relationship.

Truth be told this is what lead me to writing again. I had to write down every thought, every action I felt. Sometimes I would be up late night writing, praying and collecting my thoughts.

I must have talked all of my girlfriend's ears off till I am sure they just wanted to tell me. Girl get a life and leave that looser alone. But they were very supportive. And with a lot of prayer to God to show me and reveal to me this mans true colors towards me.

One day I woke up and he was no longer a part of my life. I could now move on to having the future that GOD promised me once I broke loose from the drama of the relationship.

Also if men you allow to enter into your life are not what you are looking for in a man why continue to date this man. It's obvious he is and never will be the type of man you need nor want and if he does change it won't be for you it will be for another woman that comes along and sweeps him off his feet. And actually you might want to consider yourself lucky.

To date a man just for the sake of having someone is really not good because it only fills your loneliness for a short time but it can also leave you feeling hurt, sad, depressed and confused and worst off than you were before you met him.

I know all this is easier said than done. Unfortunately I have been down this worn path way too many times myself but God will see you through whatever pain you are going through.

Just know that if he brought you to it. He will surely bring you through it. And on the other side of all of that will be blessings waiting for you to receive. God will give you strength every minute upon the hour if you believe and trust in him.

After all I had gone through and after all the pain I suffered I refused to let the way someone treated me be a deciding factor as to my happiness.

I learned to pray for people that hurt you, use you and abuse you. I learned to live peaceably with all men and if you go to that person and try to make peace and they don't except it that not only will you have peace you will gain their peace also.

One more thing I learned to never ever hold onto anger. And anyone who remains angry with you after you have tried to make peace with them they are giving you power over them. I don't know about you but I don't want anyone having power over me.

I knew that God had a plan to free me from the bad relationships I had chosen. Because Gods mighty hand has favor over my life each and every day.

Knowing if I stayed in faith during even the most difficult times in my life that God was going to bless me all the more. That he was going to bring supernatural favor into my life, that he was going to bring supernatural breakthroughs into my life.

I knew that God would free me from the pain, depression and sadness I felt each and every time I choose to make a bad decision.

Today because I choose not to let situations control my life. I am at peace. I am happy everyday. I have a smile on my face everyday.

I try to bring joy to ones life not sadness and if by some chance I do hurt someone I go to that person and apologize and try to make peace. I never hold onto anger. I know this is the only way to live and the only way I want to live.

Today I am happy with myself and have the strength and confidence through GODS grace to get me through every single day. After all I am a beautiful, smart, woman with a lot to offer. And no one can hold me back but me.

By no means am I proclaiming to be an expert or to know it all I am just speaking on my own true life experiences.

Believe me since I am human I still make mistakes but I always have to go back to what I know and that is the word of God and his direction for my life. I am hoping that my stories will help someone.

Somehow I am hoping that my poetry will bring a smile to many, that my poetry may bring strength to others, that my poetry may bring confidence and hope to ones life. All I know is I was inspired to tell my story and all of this is truly From the Bottom of My Heart.

# I Feel

I feel so lonely all the time but what I really want
Is a love I can call mine

I feel sad more times than often and I feel that sometimes
my feelings are forgotten

I feel sometimes all alone and I cry myself
to sleep till those feelings are gone

I feel sometimes that things are out of control
I have to pray to God to get me out of
this hole

I feel sometimes I take too many chances
but that's how we learn through our choices
and circumstances

# I Guess You are Right

I guess you are right God already told me he would
supply all my needs
He told me if I have faith he will aim to please
All I wanted from you is for you to listen to my concerns
I believe at
Least that respect I should have earned

God told me to let it all go he even said cry a little
No one will ever know
He said I am your friend and confidant I will be there
for you and listen to your needs and wants

Just because you are not the man you should be. Does
not mean God is not going to send me someone so I can
Let my love run free

And when no other woman will show you this type of
love watch you come running and praying to God above

You always played games and your feelings ran hot
And cold. You cant mess with a child of God
Man you are mighty bold

When older folks tell you something you should
Really listen. My love is what you will truly be missing

Bye Bye now I gotta go. I have God waiting
For me who keeps me focused through
Highs and lows

# I had to let you go

I had to let you go so you would not be so confused
I had to let you go so I would not continue to feel so used

I had to let you go so that you could begin to grow
I had to let you go so you could take things slow

I had to let you go for so many reasons. Maybe our love was only for that particular season

I had to let you go as you walked out that door
I realized that you and I were not going to be together anymore

But that's ok I see for myself a better future and with GODS help my weaknesses he will nuture

# I Know

I know I should be patient towards all men
It's not a contest of who should win

I know I must obtain from fornication
I know I must not have certain kinds of relations

I know that I must begin to recognize. I know I must
control my anger so I don't have to apologize

I know I must not allow myself to get so close
I know this because I always end up hurting the most

# I miss you

I miss seeing you now that you are gone
I miss hearing your voice on the telephone

I haven't seen you in quite a while. I miss
seeing your silly smile

I miss your little pet names without you in
my life things just aren't the same

I miss the times we spent together
rain, shine or any kind of weather

I miss you telling me how deep your love
was. I guess I miss you just because

# Inauguration Day 2009

What I seen on the day of the inauguration. People of all ages and of all generations.
WhatIseenonthedayofinauguration.Manyfaces,people of different religions, people of many different races. What I seen on the day of inauguration people young and old. People full of glory and behind their faces stories that have never been told.

They came in from many countries. Everyone working together to fight for justice and liberty. It was people like Martin Luther King that fought to set us free.

What I seen on the day of inauguration made me want to cry it showed me what we can do with Gods grace and mercy if we have faith and try.

President Barack Obama has shown us all "Yes We Can" He has shown the American people that he wants to be our President and our friend.

The number of folks that came was astronomical
It shows what we all can do together if we are trying
to accomplish and reach the same common goal

Everyone wanting to see change in history it has been
GODS grace and mercy to set his people free.

GOD is putting Barack Obama in charge and giving
him title as President. He was the best choice for the
job that has been clear and evident.
His wife Michelle our first lady full of beauty and of
grace. She will be there by her husband's side and help
him with the challenges that this nation must face.

Our first lady has much poise and elegance. She will
be an excellent first lady since she has been given this
chance and you can see the beauty of her with just a
mere glance.

There will be many obstacles and set backs that this
world will experience. President Barack Obama
promised us he won't lie to the people and lead us
under false pretense.

I wish the people of our past history could have seen
this historical day. The joy, the gladness, the tears "OH
NO" not because of sadness. It's because of what is yet
to come. President Barack Obama has a big challenge
and today he has just begun.

I'm sure as he was sworn in God looked upon him and said "Well done my child and my friend" "I'm putting you in charge of this race. Now its time for you to begin"

God promised us the first shall be last and the last shall be first. Change is what the American people want . This is what we hunger for this is what we thirst.

Go on President Barack Obama and do the job that GOD has set in front of you.  With every challenge, with every setback, with every obstacle GOD will see you through. Just keep on praying and keep the faith because GODS word is true and if he did not believe in you he would not given this enormous job to you.

Amen
GOD we give you all the glory
COPYRIGHT: SHARON HUGHLEY

# I seen a monster

I seen a monster today he was not of the human race
It was of a man I truly loved but somehow the monster
wore his face

As I looked across and over yonder. I had to take one
more glance and my thoughts began to ponder

I took another look way a far. It was the man I truly
loved sitting at the bar

As I walked over to say hello he looked at me
but his eyes no longer had that special glow

His actions towards me were so very rude
I thought to myself is this really the same dude

As I walked away I felt like someone had thrown
several darts All I could think of " was this the man
I loved from the bottom of my heart"

Sometimes people change and for absolutely no reasons why and it takes so much out of you that you began to cry

But just keep on pushing and remain strong
And before you know it the pain will soon all be gone.

# I shall overcome

When you left me I felt an awful lot of grief now that I don't have to deal with you anymore it's actually a relief

I thought that this was something that I would not overcome but since you left I am having so much fun

Just because our relationship died did not mean I had to die with it I've learned a lot of lessons and next time I am not going to relive it

At first when you left I was angry even livid. Now I realize it was the best thing you could have done for the both of us because in you I have lost all trust

So we both made the decision before things got too out of control that we could no longer be together because we were both to emotional

# I think of You

I think of you day and night. I know our affair was not right. I can not change how I feel the love I had for you was very real

I pray that my sins will be forgiven but without you in my life its hard to keep on living

I pray that God will take these feelings away so that I can have a healthy relationship someday

In life you live and you learn and you take chances when its your turn. No matter what life sends my way I am gonna keep my faith and continue to pray

# I Use To

I use to ask GOD why am I under attack
but things could be worse I could be a person
on crack

I use to wonder why things seem so extreme
I use to wonder what life would truly bring

I use to have ways of the wicked but through
GODS grace I have truly licked it

I use to be so adamant. And carried things on to
it's full extent. I use to wonder why I felt so uncertain
but now I have given my life to GOD and I am
no longer hurting

# I waited for you

I waited for you and you were not quite what I expected
But as I got to know you I seen you were who God had
elected

I met you sometime last November it was at my moms
house. Do you Remember?

We talked on the phone off and on and since then our
relationship has truly grown

We were both involved with some one other and you
and I were never lovers

We were just friends with our hearts elsewhere we were
attracted to each other but we did not dare

As the relationships began to dissipate could this be
our chance? Or is it just fate?

To see you on the weekends I can hardly wait I'm like
a kid in high school going on my very first date

# I wanted to

I wanted to call you just to say hello but I didn't want you to think I was thinking about you I didn't want you to know

I wanted to stop by and see your face but I didn't want to be accused of just stopping by your place

I wanted to tell you how much you were missed but then I got to thinking that as usual I was always last on your list

I wanted to just call you and tell you how much I cared but after careful thinking I would not be treating myself fair

I guess I just wanted you to love me as much as I loved you but it was only wishful thinking that could possibly be true

Deep down inside my heart knew that you did not love me as much as I loved you

# Its All About Me

I am having such a blast now that I have gotten rid of you at last
Your not dragging me down anymore with those old stories of the past
Things are not as bad as I thought they were gonna be now that I have taken time to get to know me
All things works out for so many reasons and me is who I am going to worry about pleasing
It's all about me from this point on this is one of life's lessons that I had to learn on my own actually the lessons has changed my life and made me strong

# Its gonna be ok!!!!!

When things seem bleak and not going my way.
I take time to meditate and time to pray.
When life takes a turn that I think is for the worse
God shows me that I need to trust in him at all times first.
When I am down and feeling my all time low
I pray to God to give me strength to give it another go.
When finances fizzle and I don't know what is next
I remember that my God knows what is best.
With that all being said I now have the courage
And with God on my side I have no more worries.
Just look to God to heal all your hurt and your pain
With God you have nothing to loose and everything to gain.
You no longer have to worry how you will make it
from day to day
God told me to tell you its gonna be ok!!!!!

# Its time to say Good Bye

Its time for me to say goodbye. There is no sense in me hanging on there is no sense in me continuing to cry

It's time for me to say farewell. My love for you was real couldn't you tell

I don't know why you just couldn't tell me you wanted to be with your wife. Why didn't you just tell me that she was your everything she was your life.

God has plans for me so I am not scared. Life doesn't always treat us good life is not always fair

I wish you well and don't want to see you hurt Its time for me to leave you alone and stop putting up with all your dirt.

Goodbye Goodbye go on your way. I am not going to let you keep me miserable I want to be happy someday

# Jesus Unfailing Love

When all earthly supports and emotional holds disappear. Reach to GOD he will hold you near.

Jesus loves us and comforts us through all eternity even when we have immature thoughts and low mentality.

Jesus unfailing love has been there through all my difficult times and through his grace and mercy he is surely one of a kind.

I have been in so many terrible situations. Accept GOD as your savior. You don't need an invitation with you he wants to have a relation.

He listens to my hurt, pain and heartaches.
GOD has gotten me through some rough times for goodness sakes.

Jesus is my constant companion and my dearest friend. His love never fails me he has certainly made that clear. He will be there till the very end with him I can be myself and never have to wonder if I still have a true friend.

# Last Chance

Some things I hate to mention but I know you had really good intentions. Things to me still ain't right I'm still sleeping by myself every night.

I'm the one showing all the initiative and to me you still seem really unappreciative

Then you say we can't keep tearing each other apart. It would not have been this way If you had been upfront with me from the start

I wonder if you would understand. If you would put yourself. In my shoes if you did maybe we would not be at the point that we had to choose

The whole thing is and what I take offense is that you got me to be with you under false pretense

# Last Night

Last night you lay next to me with no sex involved
Our bodies touching and caressing with no care in the
world at all
The passion that we felt we wanted it to last. We did
not let troubles bother us no not even our past. Our
souls were connected as we shared our love and our
affection
The passion between us was ever so sweet as our bodies
began softly to gently meet. As our bodies pressed
close to each other we both said we did not want to be
with another
We awoke to the light of the shining sun. We had no
regrets no not even one

# Learn a Lesson
# from the Lesson

I have a confession messing with people like you
I know I have truly learned my lesson

Next to God above I was the one who showed you real love

How could you belittle someone like me to others.
Did you care about my life did you care about my
struggles I am moving on with my life because you are
a backstabber. And I can still feel the knife

The devil is not going to steal my joy. I am not going to
let you treat me as if I am some worthless cheap toy

For now on you I am going to ignore you are not my
life and new opportunities I must explore

Maybe before I just wasn't getting it but with you
anymore I am not with it

86

# Lets be Friends

Lets just be friends my love for our relationship have come to an end I only want you around for my needs I don't care about you nor do I am to please.

What you feel and think is dumb why cant you just be there for me to listen to my problems

I'm going through a lot of things right now. With your wants and needs I am not down. I know I sound like a selfish man. I should care about you because you have truly been my friend.

That is just too much to ask I just want you to do what I say. And maybe we can be together again someday.

I don't care about you right now. I don't even care if I hurt you or how these words may sound. With you right now I am just not down.

I have so many things right now on my plate with you right now. I just can not relate. Lets just be friends with no strings attached. Right now I am not good for you I am not quite the catch.

As you can see once again it's all about me and what I am going through has made my heart heavy. Two woman I can't handle anymore I don't know what to do and I wonder what did I let myself get in this situation for.

I am sorry I can't be there 100% for you. Go ahead and do what you want. Stop trying to convince me I will never see your point.

As I said before you have been there for me but I still have blinders over my eyes cant you see. And you and I will never agree.

Bye Bye my love I must leave you alone. I told you before my feelings for you are gone and I just want to be left alone. I hope my marriage I have not truly blown because my heart really wants to go back home.

# Lets get it on in 2008

Lets get it on in 2008. This is my motto can you
Relate. Sometimes I wonder is this all really true
I'm still living with this guilt and I don't know what to do

I keep playing things over and over again
Lord will you just forgive me for I have sinned

All this stuff all bottled up in my mind
Maybe in 2008 things will be different this time

Maybe if I move and get away from the drama
I can clear my mind and heart from everyday life's trauma

I'm having such a hard time moving on
And this pain just seems to keep dragging on and on
Lord please help me for I know I did wrong

I know I kept being stepped on like someone's door
mat. But I can't stop thinking what life use to be like
before this and that

Gosh can't you just love me like I have loved
You. Why does our love have to be over why does it
have to be through.
Will you tell me if there is anything I can do my heart
is with you and I do love you

Lets get it on in 2008 this is to all who can really and
truly relate. Lets get it on in 2008

# Letting Go

Letting go is so hard to do especially when you love some one more than they love you.

Letting go brings so much heart ache and so much pain it makes you feel you have everything to loose and nothing to gain.

Letting go is hard to do for it brings so much sorrow But look to God he will bring you through yet another tomorrow.
God said don't you fret, don't you fear. I am here to wipe away all your tears.

Yes letting go is hard to do but have faith in God and he will see you through. All your hurt and all your pain will soon turn for your prosper and your gain.

If you feel weary and at the end of your rope look to God and he will give you hope. Through God he gives you light to get you through yet another night.

Don't let go of loving again believe in God as your trusted friend.

God will give you the desires of your heart just follow him down the path for a fresh new start. So letting go may be hard to do but now just have faith and strength from God to get you through.

Letting go is hard to do even if you were the one who said we were through.
What hurt the most is I was your friend I was with you through thick and thin.

A love so kind so ever new now its gone and now were are through.
God gave us the opportunity to go through new open doors now your gone forevermore

I thought that love was the answer, I thought love was the key now its just shared memories of you and me.

# Life's Trails

Isn't it funny how life takes you down different trails
one path I don't want to take and that's the trip to Hell

Isn't it funny how some days your up and some days
your down and all you want to do is turn your life around

Isn't it funny how some people have nothing and some
people have everything. Isn't it funny what life often
brings

Isn't it funny how life bring so many challenges
Isn't it funny how life has A way of balancing

Isn't funny how one day you are on this kingdom
and then the next day you are locked up and lost your
freedom

But keep on pressing and pay attention God is waiting
for you if I failed to mention

# Life's Turns

When life seems to take a turn for the worse
Remember that our Savior went through this first

He died on the cross to save our souls
What he went through no body really knows

As he's nailed to the cross and bearing all of our pain
I wonder what he must have been thinking and if the
people watching beared no shame

What a heavy load for Jesus this all must have been
To try to save our souls and the remission of our sins

What a lovely man I hope to meet him some day
When its time to walk through the pearle gates
I hope God says
"Let her in she's ok"

# Live your life without me

He told me to leave him and live my life He said its not
you sweetheart I already have a wife

He said maybe someday we could give it another try
He said he would find no one better than I

He told me he was hurting very much inside he said
there is no excuse as to his reasons why

He said it was going to hurt him to see me go as to why
he has made certain decisions nobody really knows

He told me that sometimes he wish he would just die
My heart poured out to him as we both began to cry

I love you and this is very much true. My heart will
always be with you

# Looking Back

Looking back way back when. Things were good between us
"Well yes that was then" Now we have grown so far apart. My heart always loved you from the very start.

I remember when we would dance
and I would think "Thank you Lord for I have finally got real love. I finally got my chance."

To love someone with all I have got.
But then the arguments started and we just fought and fought.

It broke my heart into tiny pieces. But that was your way out that was your release. Because to someone like me you were unavailable but it still left my heart into tiny pieces that were untraceable.

I prayed to GOD so many times "Why did I fall for a man of this character a man of this kind" All he ever did was lie to me no matter how hard I tried.

I felt so embarrassed when we parted and so ashamed. I realized its no one else's fault I am the one to blame. So I asked GOD to please release me of this awful pain.

One day I woke up and you were no longer on my mind. Next time I will be more careful not to fall for a man of your character a man of your kind.

# Lord

Lord I need your wisdom and understanding in my daily life affairs
Lord you said that you would not put any more on me in my life than I can bare.

Lord thank you for strengthen me from daily life's challenges and circumstances
Lord thank you for holding my hand and leading me down the right path when I needed guidance.

Lord if it wasn't for you there would be so many obstacles that would have been difficult for me to overcome. Lord I thank you that I am one of your children.

Lord so many times my life seemed so dismantled. But Lord I decided that through your grace and mercy any situation that came about I should be able to handle.

Lord you held me close and my soul and mind you nurtured. Lord if it wasn't for you I would not have been able to see my future.

Lord as I listened to you and began to hear your voice. Wrong decisions were no longer an option they were no longer my choice.

Lord now everywhere I look I see beauty and possibilities. Your grace and mercy shine upon me and with my choices now I hope that you are pleased.

Lord I am so glad I no longer have to live my life in seclusion. Lord it took some time for me to see that I just needed your divine solution.

Lord for me you gave your life and suffered much pain. You did that freely with nothing in mind to gain. So Lord to you every area in my life I give and I do surrender. Lord help me to be a better person and to be less of a sinner.

Lord please help me to be a better Christian. Lord I'm crying out to you asking that you continue to forgive me for all my sins. Lord let your light continue to shine on me as my new life begins.

# Lord Guard my Mouth

Things more and more are becoming so Mi nute
And I am not going to continue to argue. I just will not
contribute

How come we can't agree to disagree instead of staying
mad and angry

I would like to bless others with my tongue and stop
cursing out everyone

Were are making the devil proud by yelling and arguing
and talking out loud

Lord I am trying to make things right. Lord give me
grace to say things that bring people life

# Lord help

Lord send your love on all the unjust
This is my prayer request this is a must
Lord help those who are on the wrong paths of life
Relieve them of the pressures of daily strife.
Lord help those who are in pain right now
Lord help those who feel really down
Lord help those who can't seem to get it right
Lord help those people to see the light
Lord this is just my prayer request
Thank you Lord
You are the
Best

# Lord you said

Lord you said you would hold no good thing
From me. Even though I'm a sinner am I really worthy

Lord you said you would be my strength
When I am weak. Lord I need your strength right now
while I feel so timid and so meek

Lord you said there is the kind of friend
That sticks closer than a brother. Thank you
God for I would truly want no other

Lord you said faith is the substance of things
Hoped for. Trust in God and you will
give us our hearts desires

Lord you said if you be for me who shall be
Against me. Thank you Lord for in
You I do believe

Lord you said for with the mouth confession
Is made unto salvation.
Lord I thirst for you and to have with
You a deeper relation

Lord I just can't thank you enough for the
Blessings the open and closed doors
And even the times that appeared so rough

Lord I just truly want to magnify your name
Lord forgive me for my sins
Of which have caused me so much shame

# Loves Mistake

Was your love for me real or fake or did you feel our relationship was a big huge mistake

Sometimes I wonder what our love was really about
I know I was in love with you without a shadow of a doubt

You always said I was a breath of fresh air. But when I needed you most you were not there

Do you know about real love or have you no clue
I don't really care anymore with you I am through

Some people feel that love is pain. If you really believe that you really are insane

After all you put me through I have found this to be true I wonder how could I have possibly ever fallen in love with you

# Memories

All of the memories of what use to be. Tender kissing
from you to me
You were never mine from the start. I'm not blaming
you I too did my part
If you had been really true about me and you. We would
have stayed together and no where near through
Life with everything else has its purpose starting over
again made you really nervous
I don't know why you had to pretend that you were my
trusted friend
I am glad I was put in your life to help you with what
you needed
I was only suppose to be with you for that particular
season
I too learned lessons and I too got out of the relationship
what I needed
Good Luck to you we will meet again but next time I
would not have choosen you as a trusted friend

# My brothers and my sisters

My brothers and my sisters have always been so encouraging
My brothers and sisters love have been so nourishing

My brothers and sisters were there in times of assistance. Even if I tried to refuse their help and show some resistance

I have so much fun when I am with my sisters and brothers. We laugh and joke and talk about when we were children

Brothers and sisters I love all six of you
I hope you all feel the same about me too.

God Bless you all
Take care

# My Church

I joined my Church sometime in nineteen Ninety Four
since I joined as a member God opened so many doors

Since I joined I began to step out on faith and not by
sight some things in my life just wasn't quite right

The Lord continues to give me grace to keep me
grounded. Listening to the Pastors message weekly
also helps keep me well rounded

I pray for the continual growth of my Church and
remember brothers and sisters in Christ that God loved
us first

# My closest friend

Next to God my mother is my closest friend
She is the one I talk to when all my relationships come
to an end

My mother held me strapped to her back my mother is
the one who kept our family intact

My mother is the one I could always count on
my mother always knew when something was wrong

My mother is the sweetest peach on my tree. My mother
has my back please believe me

My mother is the one to keep me in line. My mother is
the dearest woman you will ever find.

# My dad

I remember being a little girl and wanting to get my
dads attention

My dad is a lovely man in case I failed to mention
I remember my dad being such a strong man
I remember my dad doing for his children whatever he can

My dad is someone who will not take no ones mess
My dad is always going to tell you the truth about
yourself. With him you will never have to guess

What I am trying to say is my dad is a good man
He is the best dad that GOD could have sent.

# My feelings for you

I am sorry I was not there for you while you were ill.
I needed to get my thoughts together I had to take
time to chill.
Your love at one time I truly did treasure but please
understand I was under so much pressure. Because of
my selfishness I knew you deserved better but I kept
you to myself instead of giving you the goodbye letter.

Meeting you I now have regrets. I know I paid not
enough attention to you and you I did neglect. For you
I had such a terrible passion and because of greed. I
could not let you go. I could not even tell you my true
feelings I could not let you know.

But I am not playing with you anymore games my
feelings for you are just not the same. This is the fact
that still remains. I am not man enough to tell you this
to your face. So I will just disappear without a trace.

I will tell lies on you to everyone and make myself look good. For I have no respect for you and my wish is for you to leave me alone

You held my hand but my heart you could not fully reach. You wanted 100% of me but my mind was not complete. You did touch my heart in so many ways and you showed me how a man should be treated and kept my love for you at bay. You were the memory keeper and you kept me in your heart. But our affair was not something we should have start.

# My Ideal Man

I want a man who will be on my team
Not listen to other folks and know It's me he believes in.

I want a man who will be there
For me when I am feeling ill
Rub my back and let me know his love Is real

I want a man who communicates
One who I can trust and one that relates

I want a man who will be on my team
Not put me down and treat me mean
instead build me up and one who I can truly love and trust

I want a man who is a man of God
Who knows how to treat me and one who knows
That cheating is not allowed

I want a man who I can be really proud
One who dresses nice and dresses in style

Bottom line I want a man with
All these qualities once he finds me it will be
Such a relief

He will be a man GODLY and sincere
he will be a man that will have no fear a man that will
hold me dear

# My Mind

My mind is constantly going as I am going through stuff. I have had some hard times actually I have had it rough

My mind is finally at peace and I don't think of you much anymore to say the least

My mind has seen people come and go. My mind has been at its all time low

My mind is just patiently awaiting. And to God my life I give and dedicating

# My Prayer

God I am asking for peace and mercy to my soul.
What I have been through in life no one actually knows.
Lord I choose to follow you this very day.
Lord please save me my soul don't delay.

Lord I know I must continue to trust in you and
May I reflect goodness in all that I do. Lord let me work with
Joy and not complain. I will pray for everyone just the same.

Lord I am staying faithful and positive in my prayers.
Lord please continue to keep your hand in all of my daily life affairs.

# No more tears

I have cried so many tears as I look back over the years
I have learned that my feelings are my feelings. God is
blessing me today with spiritual Healing

Learn a lesson from the lesson since I learned that
there is no more guessing. I have finally begun
to enjoy being alone. And I also learned that loving
someone is not wrong

All you can do is give all you can give and if they don't
appreciate you learn how to forgive. Don't hang onto
anger it just causes more pain. I have to tell the truth
I'm not embarrassed nor am I a shame

# No more Temptation

I use to wonder what life would bring
Often times I felt like I had nothing

On my face I could not fake it
And my heart felt like I could no longer Take it

I often wonder what is going to happen next
As I look back on my life and took time to reflect

If I could go back and retract
I am sure some people and things in my life I would
not attract

The devil will keep you in his trap
and you might not like certain situations or how
You might react

So I am hear to tell you tell Satan
to get behind you and the next time you
Are tempted you will know what to do.

# No ordinary Joe Blow

You say you are no ordinary Joe Blow
Actually you turned out to be worst than any
Other man I know

Life has a way of showing you
People for who they truly are
You turned out to be a coward and not my shining star

I learned a lesson from all of this
And that's be careful who you lay down with

I asked God to open my eyes
He did just that by breaking all of our ties.

I hope you understand and
Will see I'm not mad at you and will never be
I'm just glad that my find is free from you and all of
that misery

# No Weapon

In the Bible it says that no weapon formed
against me shall prosper

I know what I am talking about I am
not trying to win a grammy nor an oscar

They say there is truth in the power. I don't
want what we have between one another to truly go sour

Through GODS grace I have strength. I am going to
keep trying to walk closer to God at any length

I am not going to let negativity manifest
my faith is strong so I must protest

People are always trying to bring your self esteem
and your spirits down. I am getting rid of people like
this I don't want them around

# Not Unconditional Love

You said things about me that was not true and really mean. You tried to lower my self-esteem.

My love for you was not fake and I tell you something my self-esteem you cannot break.

You said that I was flat chested but when you had problems on my chest is where your head would rest.

You said that I was really way to small did you even care about me or my feelings at all.

I opened my heart to you and let you in just because you did me wrong I can't blame all men. But you I definitely will never trust again.

I know some man will love what I have to offer and even appreciate. I am going to take some time to myself and not date get myself together and show the next man the type of woman I am and what I have to offer is great.

I don't understand why you stayed with me for over two years and why you talked about me to family and peers. I wonder why I allowed you to bring me to tears.

I prayed to GOD everyday that he would take the love I felt for you away. I would have loved you rich or poor and even loved you all the more. I would have been with you good health or poor health.

Because that's what you do when you love at your best at least I know that is what my heart felt. I realized I had to set you free and wait to see what my GOD has planned for me.

# Nothing Coming

Your words are going in one ear and out of the other
Did you think I would give him up to be with you brother

If you thought that then you got another thing coming
When you told me to walk away man that ain't fast enough.
"I'm Runnin"

Now you realize that you made a big mistake
Well right about now all I can think of is for you to go
jump in the lake

I have truly found peace within myself
I know I won't get into this situation again with no one
else

# Our Love

I have so much love for you In my heart still remaining
you need to recognize a good woman is what you
would have been gaining

You loved me and you really did not want to let me go.
You just wish I would not rush things that I would take
things slow

I'm not the type of person to just give up and quit but
then I get mad at you and had terrible fits

Then you start being so demanding after
You told me you would try to be more understanding

Now we are together trying this thing all over again we
really must learn how to be each others best friend

# Out Of My Misery

The fact still remains I am a different person now I am not the same. "Yes people can actually change."
I use to commit sins like idolatry and yes at one given time I even committed adultery but oh my GOD he set me free. I'm not living anymore in that misery.
I was looking for love in all the wrong places in and out of different relations. I did not see GOD wanted me to be with him and for me to be patient.
It's sad my life was not changed until a tragedy.
But if it weren't for my GOD oh where would I be.
Again GOD brought me out of that misery.
I use to take things so personal. I use to get angry, irate and yes irrational. I learned how not to hold onto anger. When I do that I put my own life in danger by not letting GOD fight my enemies. I am glad GOD did not let me be because I would still be living in my misery.
Thank you GOD for coming to my rescue.
If it were not for your grace and mercy I would be through. Again GOD you brought me out of that misery. I no longer commit sins like adultery.

You know like the love stories in the fairy tales
but I was looking in the wrong places I should have
been looking to GOD for his love never fails. And to
the world my story I shall tell.

# From the Bottom of My Heart

The best kinds of friends and people a person should want around them are people who are caring and kind. We as people need to be careful as to who we bring into our life, heart and soul as a friend.

Good friends will be amazing because they will be there for you no matter what. They believe in you and will bring out the best in you.

True friendship should be one of the most intimate connections one can have. Friendship is a magnificent unique blend of affection, respect, caring, trust, loyalty, love, communication, having fun and laughing together, sharing sad times together.

Oftentimes friends share the same similar interest. Friends should be understanding and give one another the benefit of the doubt and not be so judgemental.

Not all people share the same definition of friendship. Often people for definitions of friendship based on trust, communication, different experiences they have gone through in the past. Friendship is two people sharing a mutual understanding with love and respect. The longer the friendship the stronger the bond of trust will grow between the two friends.

Friendships that I have formed comes in unique ways with unique people who I choose to have in my circle. Friends that I choose to have in my life will be uplifting, caring, giving, supportive, nonjudgemental, communicators, respectful, not gossipers, will not criticize my every move, understanding and last but not least loving.

A true friend will not be jealous of other friendships you have. Mainly because not all friends share the same interest. I have found that I have friends that I go out with to have a drink, laugh and talk. I have friends that I just call or they just call me to talk but we don't really hang out together. I have friends that I talk to pretty much on a daily or weekly basis just to see how one another is doing. There are friends that I just socialize with at work.

I understand that overtime life changes and it changes people. Be careful not to choose friends that are negative and will uplift you and not bring you down. A friend that is a judger, too dependant upon you, betrayers, those who are jealous of you well those are just a few kinds of friends that you do not want in your life they will drain your energy and that is not good for anyone. Consider those type of friends toxic and run for your life.

I was so shy as a child I never had a best friend. However it did not matter much to me if I did or didn't. However at this time in my life I know that friendship is definitely important. I try to remain friends or at least in contact with all of my friends on some type of level even if it is just once a year to say hello. I try to encourage my friends, build them up and not knock them down. A person who has found a faithful friend has really and truly found a faithful treasure.

# From The Bottom of My Heart

Listed below are several Bible verses that I read on a daily basis that really and truly got me through good times and bad times. I found faith, strength, courage, hope, joy, peace, understanding, wisdom and love reading these Bible verses. I hope they will bring to you the same which is all of what GOD promised us and more.

Be anxious for nothing, but in everything by prayer and supplication with thanksgiving let your requests be made known to God. **Philipians 4:6**

Delight yourself also in the Lord, and He will give you the desires and secret petitions of your heart. **Psalm 37:4**

And we know that God causes everything to work together for the good of those who love

God and are called according to His purpose for them. **Romans 8:28**

I am leaving you with a gift- peace of mind and heart. And the peace I give is a gift the world cannot give. So don't be troubled or afraid. **John 14:27**

A good man out of the good treasure of his heart bringeth forth that which is good; and an evil man out of evil treasure of his heart bringeth forth that which is evil: for of the abundance of the heart his mouth speaketh. **Luke 6:45**

Verily I say unto you, Whosoever shall not receive the kingdom of God as a little child shall in no wise enter therein. **Luke 18:17**

Draw nigh to God, and he will draw nigh to you. Cleanse your hands, ye sinners; and purify your hearts, ye double minded. **James 4:8**

Follow peace with all men, and holiness, without which no man shall see the Lord: Looking diligently lest any man fail of the grace of God; lest any root of bitterness springing up trouble you, and thereby many be defiled. **Hebrews 12:14-15**

For if ye forgive men their trespasses, your heavenly Father will also forgive you: But if ye forgive not men their trespasses, neither will your Father forgive your trespasses. **Matthew 6:14-15**

But the LORD said unto Samuel, Look not on his countenance, or the height of his stature; because I have refused him: for the LORD seeth not as man seeth; for man looketh on the outward appearance, but the LORD looketh on the heart." **1 Samuel 16:7**

Let the words of my mouth, and the meditation of my heart, be acceptable in thy sight, O LORD, my strength, and my redeemer. **Psalm 19:14**

A soft answer turneth away wrath: but grievous words stir up anger. **Proversbs 15:1**

Dear brothers and sisters, whenever trouble comes your way, let it be an opportunity for joy. For when your faith is tested, your endurance has a chance to grow. So let it grow, for when your endurance is fully developed, you will be strong in character and ready for anything. **James 1:2-4**

God arms me with strength; he has made my way safe. **Psalm 18:32**

Blessed is he that considereth the poor: the Lord will deliver him in time of trouble. **Psalms 41:1.**

The biblical principle is, "It is more blessed to give than to receive" **Acts 20:35**.

Blessed is the man that endureth temptation: for when he is tried, he shall receive the crown of life, which the Lord hath promised to them that love him," declared the Spirit led James **(Jas. 1:12)**

Ask and it will be given to you; seek and you will find; knock and the door will be opened to you. For everyone who asks receives; he who seeks finds; and to him who knocks, the door will be opened. **Matthew 7:7-8**

There is surely a future hope for you, and your hope will not be cut off. **Psalm 23:18**

But blessed is the man who trusts in the LORD, whose confidence is in him. **Jeremiah 17:7**

I can do everything through him who gives me strength. **Philippians 4:13**

Blessed is the man who perseveres under trial, because when he has stood the test, he will receive the crown of life that God has promised to those who love him. **James 1:12**

Trust in the LORD with all your heart and lean not on your own understanding; in all your ways acknowledge Him, and He will make your paths straight. **Proverbs 3:5-6**

Fight the good fight of the faith. Take hold of the eternal life to which you were called. **1 Timothy 6:12**

Being confident of this, that he who began a good work in you will carry it on to completion until the day of Christ Jesus. **Philippians 1:6**

Peace I leave with you; my peace I give you. I do not give to you as the world gives. Do not let your hearts be troubled and do not be afraid. **John 14:27**

A man of many companions may come to ruin, but there is a friend who sticks closer than a brother. **Proverbs 18:24**

Better is open rebuke than love that is concealed. Faithful are the wounds of a friend, But deceitful are the kisses of an enemy. **Proverbs 27:5-6**

Two are better than one, because they have a good reward for their labor. For if they fall, one will lift up his companion. But woe to him who is alone when he falls for he has no one to help him up. **Ecclesiastes 4:9-10**

Do to others as you would have them do to you. **Luke 6:31**

But love your enemies, do good to them, and lend to them without expecting to get anything back. Then your reward will be great, and you will be sons of the Most High, because he is kind to the ungrateful and wicked. **Luke 6:35**

Love must be sincere. Hate what is evil; cling to what is good. **Romans 12:9**

Love is patient, love is kind. It does not envy, it does not boast, it is not proud. It is not rude, it is not self-seeking, it is not easily angered, it keeps no record of wrongs. Love does not delight in evil but rejoices with the truth. It always protects, always trusts, always hopes, always perseveres. Love never fails. But where there are prophecies, they will cease; where there are tongues, they will be stilled; where there is knowledge, it will pass away. **1 Corinthians 13:4-8**

And now these three remain: faith, hope and love. But the greatest of these is love. **1 Corinthians 13:13**

Therefore I tell you, do not worry about your life, what you will eat or drink; or about your body, what you will wear. Is life not more important than food and the body more important than clothes? Look at the birds of the air; they do not sow or reap or store away in barns, and yet your heavenly father feeds them. Are you not much more valuable than they? Who of you by worrying can add a single hour to his life. **Matthew 6:25-27**

Let not your heart be troubled: ye believe in God, believe also in me. **John 14:1**

Come to me all you who are weary and burdened, and I will give you rest. Take my yoke upon you and learn from me, for I am gentle and humble in heart, and you will find rest for your soul. For my yoke is easy and my burden is light. **Matthew 11:28-30**

I lift up my eyes to the hills where does my help come from? My help comes from the LORD, the Maker of heaven and earth. **Psalm 121:1-2**

Trust in the Lord with all your heart; do not depend on your own understanding. Seek his will in all you do, and he will show you which path to take. **Proversbs 3:5-6**

**Daily Prayer: Matthew 6:9-13 and Luke 11:2-4.**

Our Father, Who art in heaven Hallowed be Thy Name; Thy kingdom come, Thy will be done, on earth as it is in heaven. Give us this day our daily bread, and forgive us our trespasses, as we forgive those who trespass against us; and lead us not into temptation, but deliver us from evil. Amen.

# Peace

There is nothing like having peace I don't know about you but that's my belief.
Life seems to deal us so many different cards

What's the chance of totally being happy. I wonder what are the odds

All I'm saying is that I have a piece of mind. What more could I ask for what more could I find

Peace is something that all of us need peace is something we need to succeed

Peace is knowing you did your best peace is knowing that through Gods grace you are a success

# People Turn Their Backs On You

Sometimes people turn their backs on you
And you wonder what happened to the love
You once knew

Why does things have to be this way
Dear God this is a heavy price to pay

My heart is heavy and so very sad
You were the one saying bad things about me
So why are you so mad

I now see that our friendship was not for real
I don't think you know how this really makes
Me feel

I offered you my love and my heart
To trust in you
Wasn't really very smart

I will find a way to get over this
You were never mine from the start
For me to really miss

# Per our conversation

You once told me that you were very sad
I said you should go back to your
Wife even if I get mad

You said thank you for understanding
Most woman wouldn't
Honey I was only trying to be courages
Even though I shouldn't

You struggled and struggled to make
Some decisions
Left between you and I now is
Only division

You knew in your heart your decision
Was not going to be good
But you prayed to God that you
Really wished it would

And once again they showed you
Finances is what you mean to
Me. They did not care about your happiness
And that you shall surely see.
They said do things my way or its no way at all

I am the one that wears
The pants in the family or don't you recall

# Players and Playettes

Nowadays we all want
to be playettes and players
What happened to monogamous
Realationships is there not
Anything greater

I know it sounds like I am
Hating but what happened to
One on one dating

Isn't it suppose to be one
Woman to one man
Nowadays everyone is cheating
On each other just because they can

I was starting to be in that playette
Ring going out and dating every
Handsome man I seen

Now I realize that I must stay with
One dating several anymore
Is really no more fun

With all the diseases and crap out there
I'd rather take my chances with one man that cares

# Proud of my children

My children you don't know how proud of you I am
Words just can not express mothering you I have no
Regrets and from you I expect the best nothing more
and nothing less
I pray for you all day long and I ask God to keep his
Loving arms around you all the day long
Being a single parent was not easy. I worked two-three
jobs and sometimes food was scare and measley
But through GODS grace we made it through and I am
so proud of all of you
I remember when you were growing up some things
you would say were so funny and when you got older
your mouths gave me a run for my money
But I tried to teach you that parents and adults to
respect. Because you don't want to go against GOD
and later have regrets
Sometimes you would listen and did what I said but
sometimes you. Would try to do things you way and
you seen where that lead

So you got your act together and seen it GODS way. I am thankful for that this is for what I prayed

Keep on praying and let GOD lead you down the right paths. One thing for sure you don't want to go against GODS wrath

# Quit Calling

I told you to quit calling playing with my affections
I am trying to turn my life around
In the right direction

I realized you calling that you don't want nothing
Do you have a guilty cautions
Or something?

I told you to quit calling since we must part ways
Aren't you trying to work things out with your wife
Nowadays

I told you to quit calling so we could go on
I told you to quit calling there is no need
For us to talk on the phone. I told you to quit calling
because our affair was wrong

# Some People

Some people believe because they
Have material things that they are ballin

But when they put these things in front of God
They are missing there calling

Some People believe that life is just
Not fair

But just because you don't have everything you
Want doesn't mean that God does not care

Some people don't have teachable spirits
And as far as going to church will never go near it

I am going to keep all these people
In my prayers

I was once one of those people
Who thought Life did not treat me Fair

And as life comes at you you begin to think
that thought that God does not care.

But sometimes in life we have to go through
Life changes. And our life and situations
God rearranges.

# Sometimes

The days are going by and by. I often feel insecure in our relationship because you told me so many lies

Sometimes the days seem longer and longer when we spend time together makes me feel stronger

Sometimes it seem as if I running out of time. Sometimes it seems everything will work out just fine

Sometimes it seems as if the love is just not there Sometimes I can't tell if you really do care

Sometimes I feel that what you say is sincere. Sometimes I want to just keep you near

Sometimes I feel so afraid then as the days go by and by I realize these are decisions that I made

# Stick To Your Guns

Stick to your guns no matter what you go through.
If you believe you are right and what you are saying
is true.
People will try to use you and often deceive.
Listen to your gut and what you believe.
Everyone who says they are really your friend and
they care. Watch what they do and see if they are really
there.
As I lay helplessly and all alone and old friends called
me on the telephone. I was greatful to have friends like
you. If it wasn't for your kindness I would not have
known what to do.
My new friends was there but began to fade.
If we were true friends they would not have left they
would have stayed.
I told my new friends I am not mad at you.
I told you how I feel now it's up to you.
I was not trying to be rude now you have an attitude.

It's sad that you let pride lead your life. I thought long and hard. I thought about this twice. I would rather tell you the truth and how I feel.

Instead of lying about every little ordeal.

But life is too short to remain mad at everyone.

If you really love and care for someone you would forgive

them for anything they may have said or done.

As long as you live it doesn't mean you have to forget but GOD does ask us if people do or say something to us we have to forgive.

# The Bad Seed

There is always a bad seed in every crowd they tend to be liars and they talk really loud

The bad seed child has no self confidence they lie on you and say things under false pretense

The bad seed child has no self esteem and they will not really be on your team

You can't trust a bad seed child no way no how
See what you are actually going through now

Get away from the Devils work before it brings you down. This I beg of you don't let that man come around

I'm not telling you this for no reason at all. I dealt with someone like this and he tried to make me take the fall

But GOD seen where the lies hurt my heart. So he brought. The truth to light and straight out of the dark.

# The Butterfly

I seen the butterfly circling around you I thought to myself that must be an angel of someone you once knew

I seen the butterfly with colors of orange and black
I think the butterfly knew that you were actually under attack

I think the butterfly was coming to give you comfort as your walk became closer to GODwith your best effort

As the butterfly landed on your shoulder. It was a beautiful thing in the eyes of the beholder

As the butterfly flew off and began to fly. I watched till I could see the butterfly fly high into the beautiful sky

# The Perfect Man

I'm trying to remember where this all began
It was my cousin Merv that said for you I have the
perfect man

Then his wife Jade said yes he is a nice guy. I think you
should give this man a try

Merv said this man is tall with brown eyes as for his
conversation I don't know he maybe kind of shy

Jade said no Merv she likes light skin men that's all we
see her with it seems to be her trend

Merv said this man will be good for you because he
is a friend of mine. Jade said actually I think you will
probably think he is handsome and quite fine

Now neither one of them have anything to say they say.
It's your choice since you got to have things your way

Jade said he does not treat you right nor is he fair
he'd get a divorce if he really cared.

You should kick him straight to the curb and all his
lying is absolutely absurd

# The Real Deal

Women we must all come up with a resolution.
Men these days want to play us for stupid.
I hate to see us come so far along to keep messing
with these knuckleheads that bring nothing to the table
especially since they are capable and able.
We need to learn how to walk away from men who
treat us bad. Do we stay because we are longing for a
love we think we never had?
Or do we stay out of fear? Or do we stay because our
minds are foggy and not quite clear?
Do we stay for the purpose of our children?
Or do we stay because we are looking through closed
doors of how they use to be when it all first began.
Why do we let men use us and draw our energy?
Why do we deal with men whose minds are nasty?
Why do we let men take us for granite? Why do we let
men take our virginity? Why do we let men have it?
Come on women lets be smart do not let men who

don't deserve us have our heart. Just walk away and remain strong. Before you know it GOD will send you a good man it wont take long.

This is a message to all women and even some men lets quit rushing into relationships lets learn how to be friends.

We should give ourselves time to heal. I'm not trying to hurt anyone. I am just keeping it real.

Women we need to think more of our selves
and ask and pray to GOD for his help.

# The Spell

You had me under a spell I must admit. I had to take
time to stop, think and sit

Why am I letting you put me through. This It's not
worth it and I am truly pissed

You had me under a spell everyone knew it everyone
could tell. I think I kept trying because I didn't want
us to fail

You had me under such a spell. Did you not see that
I was a lovely gal

You had me under such a spell

# This too shall pass

There were so many times when I felt so sad.
Then I remember that "This too shall pass"
In times of trouble and in times of despair
I always have a trusted friend in GOD I know that he
definitely cares.
When friends are far and very few and you feel so
alone with nothing to do
Just reach out and say a prayer then you will realize
GOD has always been there.
We all have hopes we all have dreams its never to late
so it seems.
When it feels as if all hope has gone. You will realize
that GOD has never left you alone. I know for a fact
that this is all true His son died on the cross to help a
sinner like me and you.

# Times I feel sad

Anytime when you are feeling bad think of all the good time in your life you have had

Sometimes sad memories want to creep up on you. But don't let your worries get next to you. Learn not to be so sensitive go out and enjoy life and learn to live

Sometimes we have to experience sadness but try to stay away from drama and madness.

Try to live your life with joy and enthusiasm don't listen to others smart remarks and sarcasm

Keep your head up high with the most confidence and hang around people who will encourage and give you nourishment.

Practice to be your own best friend and a motivator. stay away from folks that will hurt you and you will regret later

If you can do all these things you won't feel so sad.
keep the faith and you will see that life is not so bad

# True Friend Or Foe

When you are sick and all alone people will show you their true colors. They turn on you and sometimes it's often your sister or your brother.

When you are sick and feeling down. You find out who your friends are and who really cares and comes around.

If they are your true friend they would stick by your side. They would do things for you instead of saying they tried.

Just because you sometimes disagree is that reason enough to stay mad and treat each other and be enemies.

People often say the truth hurts. I would rather hear the truth instead of talk behind your back. I actually think that's worst.

I do appreciate some of the other things that you have done. But when they are sick you don't just leave them and treat them as if they are just anyone.

The times we shared were full of tears and full of laughter. If we were really friends you would be there now and even after.

Hold onto that anger hold onto that pride.

Would you rather have a friend that told you lies.

If you were my friend you wouldn't be mad. You would respect my opinion even though it made you mad. I myself would rather have a friend who is genuine. It's not about right or wrong or who should win.

I always have to think we may not be here the next day and I know JESUS would never handle things this way.

# True Love

Don't be afraid to let true love in
Let the love flow – Don't pretend
When our lips are touching so ever tight
I want nothing more than to be with you
everyday and every night

I love the way your body feels next to mine
Its not often you find a love of this kind
Some people never find true love for real
So don't pass it up if it's the real deal

I thought I was your shining star
But you keep pushing me away so ever far
Is it because your not use to someone like me
Who allows you to be yourself and let your love run free.

Am I no longer that breath of fresh air
Or is it that you never really ever cared
You said you prayed for a woman like me
Then why are you running away and letting me be.

I don't understand what is really going on
For you to have pushed me aside and left me alone.
Now you have a heart of stone
I still wondering whatever went wrong.

# Understanding Life's Changes

During my illness as I sit and lay here everyday.
I had plenty of time to think and time to pray.
I had plenty of time to look at my life and then evaluate.
Sometimes I thought about maybe I should just relocate.
I thought very hard and reorganized things in my life and on my shelf.
As I did all that I realized I can't run from myself.
If I wanted things to change I had to look deep down inside myself and rearrange.
I had to look to see what type of things in my life I needed to change.
This way I would not keep making the same mistakes over and over again.
This time I would change my life and pray to have less sin.
I wanted to ask GOD so many questions as to why sometimes my heart was so heavy that I just broke down and cried.
GOD told me to keep my eye on the sparrow. Keep my eye on the prize.
I could not understand why my life was going this way.

GOD said child I'm trying to save you from going astray.
At that very moment I kneeled down and wept.
GOD took all my worries, cares and concerns and my soul he kept.
That's the story of a fallen Christian back on track.
Take your cares and concerns to GOD and he will surely react.

# Unreal

It really does not make much sense to act like you love me because your emotions are fake and you are acting under false pretense

You tell people I am crazy and I am a sucker. I guess to love you I was the fool yes I was the sucker.

Wow! When you said it I couldn't believe my ears. I was the one who loved you for the past few years

You showing off and acting a complete hot mess. I asked God for discernment and he put me through this test.

God is telling me to let you go. He showed me you did not really love me. He said my child you "Gotta Know???"

Just be patient and I will send you a man that really does care. He won't do mean things to hurt you he will keep you in his prayers. This man will be sensitive. To you his life he will freely give. This man will love you from the bottom of his heart. And this relationship will surely not fall apart. But you have to remember to seek first my kingdom. Don't let others persuade you for absolutely no other reasons.

# You Are

You are a person who can go far. Reach deep inside yourself and pull out who you really are

God has made each and everyone of us special
God even uses some of us as his vessels

You are a person who I respect. You are a person who I will not neglect

You are a person who I think highly of. You are the person I prayed for and I thank God above

# You must think

That's all I ever did was try to show you love
That's all I am really guilty of

You took that love and turned it into nothing
I guess what we had to you meant nothing

I'm not going to march to your beat
You will be the one come begging and at my feet

You must think you are worth that and more
Man wait and see what plans for you are in store

You can surely bet and that's a fact
This time I think you have truly met your match

I'm not bothering you so leave me alone and stop
Leaving threatening messages on my telephone

I am done with you and this time for sure
I am watching out for me my self and I this time for sure

# You Cant Live my life

You can't live my life and I can't live yours I am not
going to allow you to treat as if I am some cheap whore

I am gonna get rid of this situation at last. You coming
over here trying to give me twenty five dollars in cash

Next time you call I am not going to be available at all
I'm not going to be the one this time taking the fall

When you needed to talk who did you run to. I listened
to all that garbage but now I am through with you

# Your Character

I seen your character and I have seen your style
Do you really think you are the golden child

You had us all fooled to think you were a cool brother
But you are truly no different than any other

But I do like the way you dress and I was digging you
man. I even liked the way you smelled and the way you
held my hand

But don't think you can go back and forth between
me and her. You better stay away from me this is my
choice this is what I prefer

# We Need

We need to move forward so that we can keep our life
in order
Its not a matter of whose at fault its what we have
learned and what we have been taught
We need to move on since we have been together so long
We need to stop with the blame we are too old for
The blame game
We need to stop with all the accusing our relationship
Is over now so that's the only thing we are loosing
We need to stop talking to other folks they think
Our relationship has been a real big joke
We need to learn how to take life for what it is worth
And start thinking about our future first.

# What use to be

What happened to the love that use to be did I change so drastically or is it that you just did not really love me for me:

Or was it you that really did not want things to remain the same or did you feel this thing between us was for your gain

I can't believe you don't really love me still after all we have been through do you not want a love that is for real and true?

I know it will take time for our hearts to heal. Our fate is in Gods hands whatever will be his will????

I am so sad that you and I are not on speaking terms what you said about me is what has me really concerned

I know you told someone that I was a crazy fool is that because I fell in love with the likes of someone like you?

They say words don't harm but they actually do especially when the words are coming from someone you thought loved you too.

# What You Want

You seem to want someone who is mean and not attentive to your needs
So go on back to bull would you do that for me please
I don't want to listen to anymore of your lies you are always lying and running out of alibi's
The ones that really love you is the ones you push away
I'm telling you man you are gonna be sorry someday
A wiseman once told me you can either be with what makes you happy or what makes you sad well I don't have to deal with you anymore so that makes me very glad. Now life goes on and I will surely benefit because I don't have to listen to you complain I don't have to listen to the words that comes from your lips

# When I needed a friend

When I needed a friend God sent you. You listened to all of my troubles and my worries and when I was sick you came to my rescue in a hurry

When I was sad you wiped away my tears and told me to trust in God with all of my fears. You said hasn't he carried you through all of these years?

While I was hurting and experiencing pain you stood beside me with nothing to gain. That's what I call a trusted friend who would stand beside me through thick and thin

God said a friend will stand closer to you than a brother. I am glad God choose you to be my friend with you I don't have to act a certain way nor pretend

There are times when we all are in such despair but I don't have to worry about our friendship I know that you are a one friend that from the bottom of your heart you really do care.

# Who Would

Divorce is one of the hardest things a person can go through. Who would have thought that things would end between me and you

Who would have thought that you would go off and leave me someday. I loved you so much I wanted you to stay.

Who would of thought that you would get so depressed who would have thought things would end up in court and would be such a mess

Who would have thought that you weren't quite strong enough. I guess not even the strongest man on earth is not so tough.

Who would have thought you would have so many things on your plate. Who would have thought you would treat me as an enemy and if I was second rate.

Who would have thought that you would feel blue.
Who would have thought that what you prayed for
would come true.

# Why didn't you tell me

I don't know why you did not tell me from the gate that all you wanted from me was me to be your playmate.

You said you wanted someone to love you and treat you right.

To love you and hold you throughout the night. You said I was one of the best friends you have ever had but when I don't do what you want all you do is treat me bad.

I thought you wanted something good out of life. But me who loved you – you stabbed in the back with a knife.

You told people that I was not of your taste. Two years we stayed together it seems such a waste. You said my breast was small and tiny. To me your attitude is small and whinny.

You said that I was a real big liar. Put me and you together and see who people really admire. I bet I will be the one coming out on top. Your feelings I'm gonna hurt so I am gonna stop.

I can't believe over you I lost sleep especially after finding out that you are a real big creep.

To me you are a real disappointment. I can't believe I loved you to any extent. At one point for you there was nothing that I would not do but that was when I thought you loved me too.

# Wrong Decisions

There were times when I ended up with the wrong man just to fill a void. But on my nerves they got and all they did was annoy.

These were the chances that I would take and the wrong decisions that I would make.

I am sure there were several good guys that I let pass me by because of age, height, looks or who even know what reasons why.

There is something I can not deny some men I would not even give them a try and those were chances that I never took. I know it sounds shallow to consider one for his looks.

So here I am going through a divorce. I am not blaming anyone it was I who made that choice. I kept on trying and ended up with more and more hurt and I let men treat and the relationships I was in did not work.

So I had to take a look at myself and make some final decisions if I should stay or leave. I wanted the hurt to stop I wanted it to cease.

Sometimes we don't always make the best choice of the chances that we are given. Oh if you don't know what I am talking about just keep on living

All I know is I wanted trust, communication and romance. I wanted a man to love me and to give our love a chance to enhance. I thought if I had that then our love with last.

All I wanted was a love quick and fast. It took me forty years to see that only GODS love will last.

The choices we make in life actually reflect who we are as a person. People often blame their life circumstances on other people. When in all actuality we choose what road and what direction our life will go in. I am not stating to be an expert but I have learned through the errors of my ways what I need to do to make better choices and to better myself as an individual.

First: I decided I needed to dedicated my life trying to be the best person that I can be and to treat others the way you would want to be treated. And part of that was guarding my mouth. I am the type of person that says what is on her mind. But I had to learn that saying what is on your mind is not always so smart. Sometimes you just have to sit back, listen, and reflect.

Second: I decided I needed to respect others and respect others space. Sometimes people just need time to themselves. I had to learn not to take things so personal.

Third: I decided I needed to stay prayerful at all times. No matter if something good or bad happens in my life. I knew I needed to keep an attitude stating "If this is the worst that can happen to me then I can get through yet another day."

Fourth: I decided I needed to do good things for others. Ex: volunteer work. Not only does volunteering make me feel good. The people whom I am helping welcome whatever I have to offer them.

Fifth: I decided that I needed to encourage others at all times. I feel an encouraging word can go a long way to someone who is not having so good of a day.

Sixth: I decided I needed to talk less and listen more. Sometimes people just want to talk. We don't know what people have gone through in their life or may be going through on a day to day basis.

Seven: I needed to be effective and efficient in all that I do. If I felt I could not do something I started thinking well I need to at least try. If I don't try how will I ever know if I can complete the task.

Eight: I decided I needed to make better choices and better decisions. I seen myself making a lot of choices and decisions that lead me down a path of destruction. Had I stopped and analyzed situations perhaps I would have made a different choice.

Nine: I decided I needed just except people for who they are and not try to change them into what I thought or wanted them to be.

Ten: I decided that I needed to choose my friends and associates more wisely. Not everyone can be your friend.

I have been homeless but never without a home with Jesus

I have been down but not out

I have been alone but never lonely with Jesus